Transforming Your Reality: Removing the Mask

Dr. Michelle Boone-Thornton

Transforming your Reality: Removing the Mask

Published by *Weird Disciple Publishing*
Edited by *Marrisa Thornton, Articulate*

© *2023 Dr. Michelle Boone-Thornton*
ISBN (paperback): 978-1-7326548-4-6

Table of Contents

Dedication

This book is dedicated to my children Courtney, Marrisa, and Virgil II. From the moment they were born each one of them has brought me indescribable joy and helped me to develop into the woman I am now. I had no idea that they were the missing component that I had searched for over half of my life. I thank God for entrusting me with each one of you. You have always provided me with unconditional love and support. Our love has no boundaries and brings out the unapologetically authentic me.

Foreword

I have known Dr. Michelle Boone-Thornton my entire life. While most call her Dr. BT, I call her mom. There are many things I can say, but I'll give an example instead. We both traveled to Kenya for the first time in July 2022. During our visit we attended a naming ceremony with a Maasai Mara tribe. The naming ceremony consisted of the person being named sitting on a short stool in front of the tribe, the tribe looking at that person, gathering together, and determining the tribal name for that person. They did this for each person. We were so fascinated because the name given is only based on the tribe looking at the person. My mom's tribal name translated to *harmony*. She was confused at first, but it was so clear to me. It's the essence of what she does and her passion to help others moving toward being their true selves. Harmony, that's who she is.

You can't have harmony if you're constantly masking who you are. Instead, you'll spend most of your time fighting within yourself, who you are versus who you are pretending to be. If you are looking for harmony within yourself, or know someone that is, this book is for you. Let's be real, you know somebody needs this, if you can't think of who...it might be you. And that's absolutely okay. As you read this book, pay attention to where masking originates. This is different for everyone, so try to find out what impacts you. Then pay attention to the suggestions provided to help unmask. If you want to lose weight you have to find out what causes weight gain, avoid/minimize those things, then construct a plan that fits you and use it to help you lose weight. The same thing goes for unmasking, find out what's causing you to mask, then address it by constructing a plan *that fits you* to help you move towards being your full authentic self.

Marrisa Thornton, ARTICULATE

In a world that often encourages us to don masks and conceal our true selves, there are those rare individuals who stand as beacons of authenticity, guiding us towards the path of self-discovery and purpose. My mother, Dr. Michelle Boone-Thornton, is undoubtedly one of those guiding lights.

As a college professor, mentor, international speaker, and advocate for mental health, she has dedicated her life to helping others shed the layers of societal expectations and find their own unique identities. Her passion for serving her community, one person at a time, is an unwavering commitment that has touched the lives of many.

This book is a testament to her tireless efforts and deep understanding of the human spirit. It offers not only guidance but a hand to hold as you embark on your journey to unmask your true self and walk in your purpose. In the pages that follow, you'll discover wisdom born of experience, compassion rooted in empathy, and a message of hope that Dr. Boone-Thornton has shared with her students, her community, and, most importantly, with me.

May this book be a source of inspiration, encouragement, and the gentle push you need to embrace your authentic self. Through her words, my mother extends her hand to you, ready to walk beside you on your path to self-discovery. It's a privilege to introduce you to the wisdom of a remarkable woman, my mother, and an even greater privilege to witness her unwavering dedication to the betterment of others.

With love and gratitude, Courtney Thornton

As the publisher of this book, I want to first thank you for choosing our production. It may seem a little biased for me to put in a good word about its contents, so I will instead tell you what you can expect as you prepare to read.

Dr. Michelle Boone-Thornton herself is a well of compassion, knowledge, and wisdom. She has guided many, young and old, myself and my siblings included, down the path of mental renewal and spiritual empowerment. In all of the literature she releases, she tucks a tiny piece of her soul into the pages.

You will experience her compassion in the genuineness of her writing style and the transparency of her anecdotes. You will experience her knowledge as she reviews various statistics, scientific studies, and cognitive concepts. You will experience her wisdom as she blends together all of these elements in an easy-to-understand yet true and raw narrative.

Please relax, enjoy, and open your mind to be transformed.

Warm Regards, Virgil Thornton II

Introduction

When writing this series, *Transforming Your Reality: Removing the Mask*, I asked God to help me develop the teacher in me so that I would be able to engage children and adult learners around the world by addressing "Why" masking is a key culprit in our current mental health condition and how it is exacerbated by our, background, nationality, culture, gender, and a multitude of other variables.

I examined ways to integrate mini lessons and opportunities for self-examination and learning into my workbook, *Transforming Your Reality: Removing the Mask a Workbook*. In an in-person or virtual classroom I may start the learning process with an interactive or hands-on activity or scenario. I used the Do-First model in my workbook to help users understand "Why" they struggle and continue to bury or hide their emotions daily. Before I dive into all things unmasking, I first want to give you some background on experiences that exposed me to masking and inspired me to research, analyze, and create the unmasking process.

While in my social work undergraduate program I started to think about how I would make a difference in the lives of those whose voices had been silenced due to oppression, poverty, and invisibility. After graduating and working with children and families I realized that mental illness does not discriminate, that the stigma still exists, and that achieving a state of peace and emotional wellbeing had nothing to do with one's financial position in life. Although most families and individuals that I worked with would tell me that they just wanted to be happy, I quickly realized what they were seeking was peace.

According to the National Institute of Mental Health, in 2020, 52.9 million American adults suffered from a mental health issue. Unfortunately, these numbers only represent a segment of the population in treatment and the few who were willing to admit that there's a problem. In the 21st century, mental health is still stigmatized, misunderstood, and ignored by many. I have heard it described as an illness that weak-minded and easily influenced people get.

I am always intrigued by people who fall prey to toxic positivity and think that everyone should be able to change their mind-set, think positive thoughts and be emotionally healed. Like somehow pain, neglect, abuse, rejection, shame will just pack up and leave because you "think happy thoughts." Now do not misunderstand, I do believe positive thinking and affirmations support and help maintain a healthy lifestyle. These Jedi mind tricks do not work without action on your part. As with your physical health you must incorporate healthy eating, exercise, meditation, medication, doctors, physical therapists, massage therapists, etc. Mentally, we need support too!

I personally have a mentor, coach, and minister that I talk to and get advice from regularly. And yes, when I worked primarily in the field of mental health, I had a therapist. You see you can't process all of your clients' problems and concerns within yourself (some situations are horrific) and you hold all of that in day-in and day-out without an outlet of your own. Now, because of confidentiality, I never shared any client specifics and mainly discussed the vicarious trauma I felt emotionally while assisting my clients.

The American Counseling Association states, "Vicarious trauma is the emotional residue of exposure that counselors have from working with people as they are hearing their trauma stories and become witnesses to the pain, fear, and terror that trauma survivors have endured." My children probably never understood why I would come home and go to my room for an hour before engaging with them. When

I lived in Alabama, I drove an hour to and from work; it was a 2-hour round trip. This gave me time to debrief myself and decompress before going home and engaging with my family. I never wanted to transfer negative energy, emotions, or feelings onto them.

After receiving my social work degree and working in the field for a few years, I pursued additional education and received a Master's in Guidance and Counseling and a doctorate in Educational Psychology. I wanted to broaden my skills and knowledge in an effort to be more effective in my approach to assisting families. The programs that I initially worked in were community-based. I sought out resources to help me provide collaborative and comprehensive services to meet the needs of my clients. Although many of my clients were children, their family and eco systems included an array of members who played a role no matter how small in raising them.

Like other illnesses, behavioral and emotional, mental health has some phenomenal caregivers. Especially when it comes to the commitment and courageousness of the grandmothers I met, who despite their own physical health conditions, would commit to raising their grandchildren whose parents were incarcerated to keep the children from entering the foster care system. Some of these children had been abused and neglected; as a result, they struggled with abandonment, rejection, and attachment issues as well as with defiance, conduct, and hyperactive disorders to list a few.

I quickly learned that community-based efforts were subject to gaps in service due to scheduling, missed appointments, transportation, and a multitude of other issues. However, I found that working with children through the school systems where they spent the majority of their day provided me with consistent access to them where I could ensure that Individual Educational Plan accommodations were implemented, and I could reinforce the interventions and skills that were provided.

One of the basic interventions I used when treating clients was identifying emotions. In fact, students in lower grades are familiar with these emotions and stickers which are used to describe the type of day *(behaviorally)* that they had at school. It is said that most humans experience about eight different emotions in a day. These emotions have several variations and nuances and can be experienced and often explained in levels of difficulty.

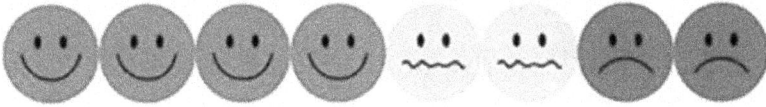

Positive

Joy - most children and some adults call this happy.

Positive or negative (seen as either good or bad)

Surprise - also labeled as pleasantly unexpected or as Mabel King sang in the Broadway play the WIZ (Don't nobody bring me no bad-news).

Anticipation - also labeled as something coming that can be good or excitement, or bad, doom, or gloom.

Trust - labeled as dependable and reliable, believable, caring or a set-up or trap, having ulterior motives.

Negative

Sadness - adults often use this emotion instead of depression.

Fear - also labeled by children as scared, adults describe it as anxiety, dread, horrified, terrified.

Disgust - I have mothers who label this as: sick and tired of being sick and tired; other statements used "I am done or over it."

Anger - children and adults also labeled this as mad, upset, frustrated, disappointed and adults describe it as foolishness or drama. Other statements include "I can't stand it," don't like, and-or could physically hurt.

I learned that children had difficulty identifying emotions and their feelings, and adults did too. When asked, many found it difficult to communicate their feelings and emotions and became uncomfortable when I pushed the issue. I heard statements like *you can't go back and change the past, no need and crying over spilled milk, why dig-up painful memories, that's just going to get everybody all upset, we have got enough drama to deal with every day.*

I knew I had to introduce this subject in a way that let everyone know that, as it relates to our mental health, we all have emotional baggage that we have been conditioned to hide and uncovering these emotions are key to achieving and maintaining emotional wellbeing. In the following chapters, I will explain this phenomenon and share the many reasons why we mask our feelings and how society reinforces this practice. I know and believe first-hand that God prepares us for our purpose. He uses everything that we have experienced in life, both trials and tribulations to accomplish his mission. We just need to look for the lessons because God is a masterful teacher.

The Process

Both the workbook and the companion journal are key components in the process of transformation, which is removing the mask. It is important that the readers understand the significance of these tools and that this book is to be used as the anchor in the series. It helps the reader not only understand why we mask, but that masking is an unwritten commandment in our society. You will be able to align with many of the stories that are shared in each chapter.

Journaling alone may not be sufficient for addressing trauma. I recommend seeking professional support from therapists or counselors who specialize in trauma therapy to ensure a safe and effective healing process. At the end of each book, you will find a resource directory that is not inclusive of every resource available but provides enough information that can help in your journey of becoming your authentic self.

The Workbook – *Transforming your Reality: Removing the Mask a workbook*

In this series the workbook was developed first because it is a crucial step, the first step towards removing the Mask. Removing the mask involves a transformation so powerful and life changing that it requires work and understanding on our part. We must address painful situations in our lives. There will be a change in our thoughts, behaviors, and attitudes. The transformation encompasses our mental health, emotional wellness, and spirituality. It is ultimately a way of decluttering, removing the negative voices, distractions, destructive patterns, and self-imposed stress. The work we do *(preparation)* prior to the transformation is what signals the change in our hearts and our minds *(thinking)*.

Using the workbook marks the beginning of the preparation process to uncover what is under the mask. It also demonstrates that we are ready for an intervention. Through the lessons and scenarios in the workbook, you will be prompted to face even more doubt, shame, guilt, abandonment, betrayal, and the pressure and conviction of what others will think, and-or what will be said about you. Who will walk away, leave you, abandon you. Or better yet, who will remain? Will it be your closest friends, your family, your spouse, or children?

Remember, you have been hiding some aspects of the truth of "the real you" for quite some time. You see the enemy will do anything he can to make you give-up, give-in, and quit. To keep you in the bondage of your own trauma. Yes, trauma! What remains trapped inside of your mind feeds your brain and traumatizes you. This is why I believe people *(many of whom seem to have a perfect life)* commit suicide, or even cut and mutilate themselves. It is a way to release the toxins caused by the mounds of negative emotions that are trapped underneath the masks they wear.

Unfortunately, masking is like a snowball rolling down a snow filled mountain side. It becomes an avalanche that may have started as just a way to cover a few character flaws that morphs into everything that has ever happened bad in life to include how someone was mistreated and-or how someone has mistreated others, bad decisions made, lies, manipulations, it's all underneath the mask.

The workbook gives you the steps and guidance that you need to defy the bondage of the mask so that you can breakthrough to the next dimension. During my workshops the books in the series are used in their entirety. Many of the participants have told me that when they attended the first workshop, they felt buried, like the emotions that they had been hiding from themselves and others. Over time they could see the transition taking place in their own lives and began to realize that they were not just going through the motions, but rather that the activities and interventions in the workbook helped them take a closer look at what was underneath their mask.

Some of us have been masking hurt, pain and a multitude of feelings and negative emotions for years. It is not until we start to peel back the layers in a therapeutic supportive setting that we gain the strength and the courage to confront what has our authentic self-hidden. Masking can affect the way we see the world. In addition to masks, some of us, erect walls around our trauma and process everything that happens in our lives (even good) through that lens.

Have you ever met someone who can't take a compliment? When you tell them how good they are there is always a ...yeah-but. Or perhaps there's that person who is always skeptical of any good deed, again there's that yeah-but...

21

There always has to be some ulterior motive. When you try to do something good for them, they may thank you, but it is quickly pointed out what else you could have done or something that you did not do.

The workbook is an in-depth emotional wellness process. As a college instructor, I like to present learners with the opportunity to understand the "Why"- is this relevant to me. The scenarios and activities in the workbook provide users space to not only write about their emotions and feelings but most importantly read and re-read, identify, and measure their vulnerabilities. Our vulnerabilities are what we struggle each day to mask, cover-up, and hide from the world, our friends, families, and ourselves. Don't be afraid to use this workbook!

In a season where many of us are concerned about our overall physical health, such as actively adjusting our diets, exercising to reach goals that impact our weight, heart, cholesterol, A1C, blood pressure and more, we should also put just as much effort into our mental and emotional health. Use this workbook, companion journal, and self-help book as your daily emotional wellness check-up and adjust as needed to reach your goals.

The Companion Journal – *Transforming your Reality: Removing the Mask – Companion Journal*

The companion journal was the second component that was developed in the series. Out of the abundance of the heart the mouth speaks, and these words, thoughts, and actions should be captured in the journal. It is important that you write about your newfound strengths, the positive messages that now replace the hurtful ones. When you write it out it becomes engrained in your heart and what's in your heart becomes the messaging in your mind. The act of writing, rewriting, reading, and re-reading reinforces it all.

This journal can be used to chronicle and tell the story -- your story -- of how you found the free and uninhibited you. You will find that you are no longer bound by anything but living the life and following the plan for your life that God has for you. It was in place before you were formed.

Other benefits of journaling include:

- A safe and private space to express emotions that may be difficult to share verbally which can be cathartic and provide a sense of relief.
- It encourages self-reflection, self-growth, self-awareness, self-compassion, and introspection.
- Helps you gain a deeper understanding of your thoughts, feelings, reactions, and even triggers.
- Writing helps you distance yourself and create a perspective that makes it easier to process and make sense of the trauma.
- It allows you to release the hidden pent-up emotions and stress. Writing about challenging or distressing experiences can serve as a form of emotional release, helping to alleviate feelings of anxiety, sadness, or anger.
- It can help you organize your thoughts and problem-solve. Many of my clients have said that they have trouble sleeping because thoughts are racing in their head constantly. By putting thoughts into words, you can gain a new perspective on what you perceive as challenging and find potential solutions.

- It can also serve as a way to set new or reformatted goals using a S.M.A.R.T. formula, visually track your progress, and identifying patterns or triggers in other words what causes you to react/ behave/ or feel a certain way (anxious, nervous, guilty etc.).

It is important to note that while journaling can be therapeutic, it may not be suitable for everyone. If you are experiencing severe emotional distress or mental health concerns, it is recommended to seek professional help from a therapist or counselor.

Transforming Your Reality: Removing the Mask

This book will educate you, help you take charge of your destiny, and seek answers and knowledge about masking. It can change the trajectory of your life. We all need some kind of help or assistance in some area of our lives. No man is an island! I have intentionally published this book last in this series. By using the workbook and journal first, this allows users to begin the process of uncovering specific issues in their lives, addressing them, and then helping them understand how and why we mask emotions so they can show up as their authentic self in every aspect of their life.

The combination of all three components in the Transforming Your Reality package is my way of providing not just the tools but the resources that you will need in this process. In some of the chapters, I have added interventions and strategies that have been researched and found to be effective methods for helping you improve and maintain a state of emotional wellness. In the appendix you will find a list of mental health resources, surveys, checklists, and assessments that I encourage you to use as needed.

The Pressures to Mask

The Mask

If you are like me, you have people in your life who feel that it is your responsibility to fix everything for them. They never ask you how you feel, if you need anything, or if they can help you in any way. I think that masking creates this insensitivity towards your own needs *(for yourself and others)* because you always act like or are masked to look as if everything is in control. It's as if everybody else except you can feel bad or have a horrible day.

I remember one day in particular going through my normal routine getting to work, dropping off kids-picking up kids, cooking dinner, washing clothes, and jumping in my car to drive 25 minutes out-of-my way to give someone a ride to a meeting we were supposed to attend because she didn't like driving but wanted to go. When I got to her house, she said, "I got a headache so I'm not going." I thought to myself, "you didn't bother to call me to let me know."

We live in a world that's full of adversity, trouble, problems, and heart ache. We will all have trials, tests, and challenges, as well as good times. We must understand that God is perfect, not us. We were not created to be all things to all people all the time, again that's God. If you convince yourself and others that the masked image is who you are then you will start to believe it. The struggle is maintaining the lie and the emotional bandwidth that it takes to try to look happy when you cry yourself to sleep every night.

When we put on a "Happy Face" 24/7 to keep others from seeing our affliction, it sends mixed messages to us. It portrays and models an all-is-well façade to others in your community, home, workplace, church, and all throughout your environment; thereby altering your own reality.

The pressures to mask can be innate, culturally-based, and heavily influenced by society. Through the mask we can shelter and conceal our true feelings and portray more acceptable images of happiness, success, and being worry-free. For many, the struggle to fit in and be accepted is real. It is a constant battle to be something, or someone, who you are not and to maintain a façade during periods of emotional warfare.

Smile to keep from crying, put on a happy face, no worries be happy, it's all good, are popular phrases that reinforces the masking of our true feelings. Each phrase indicates that underneath is a reality of hidden emotions.

In some cases, we wear masks over our masks. Yes, we have a closet full of masks just like clothes. As women, we seem to wear a multitude of hats: wife, partner, mother, parent, single-parent, sister, employee, business owners, Soror, Church member, caregiver, cook, maid, mediator, connector, facilitator, chauffer, etc. This list is infinite.

For example, in the roles that I listed my relationship with my spouse can be strained and the struggle to stay together is ongoing, but the mask of wife looks perfect; at the same time, I may be feeling insecure about my role as a mother, but my mask of mother looks unblemished.

Masks, some are brushed and painted on and others -- invisible, closely resemble a Halloween costume that we adorn as we enter the workplace and remove once we leave. While wearing these masks we behave in a manner that both supports and reinforces the public persona or job stereotypes. In fact, some people in work environments adjust their mask as the culture and climate of their organization changes, and to appease administration or leadership.

Now we have to consider the impact of the economy, global markets, technology, and product outsourcing. They can seriously impact business and employment, creating on-going uncertainty as it relates to our livelihoods and source of income. This is a great example of the societal pressures to mask our feelings and emotions as it relates to this phenomenon.

Who wants to let others know how scared they are about the impending doom that hangs over our heads like clouds each waking day? We use concepts like imposter syndrome and code switch to support the masks we adorn at work to give the illusion that these images are who we are and necessary to navigate our work environment.

Other Forms of Masking That May or May not be Harmful

Imposter Syndrome

Every time I write about the topic of imposter syndrome, I am always perplexed. It is not always clear who is fooling whom. Is the imposter fooling others or is the imposter the fool? I have experienced both assumptions.

In the first example *(I am the fool)*: I have worked for many bosses who have a general idea about day-to-day organizational functions but relied on my skill, knowledge, and expertise to move the department forward. I was not always invited to the executive or corporate meetings; however, occasionally did attend a few.

I was often told that I was being groomed for higher-level positions and was a great team player. I would meet with my boss prior to the meeting and share my opinions, thoughts, ideas, innovations and after we'd meet would be asked to provide a bulleted synopsis of what was discussed. In the corporate meetings, I showed up wearing my corporate mask and listened as my ideas became their ideas. Whenever my boss was asked to give any specifics, during the meeting, I would be introduced as the expert in this area, or one of the team leaders on this project. *Michelle will answer any questions you have.* The thing about imposter syndrome is that you end up fooling yourself. Whenever you mask in any arena you cheat yourself.

The psychological constructs behind this syndrome are endless and can lead to people fooling themselves and often devaluing the skills, abilities, and accomplishments they do have. They have a persistent fear of being exposed as a fraud, despite evidence of their competence. It can lead to individuals masking their true feelings and devaluing their own skills and abilities. Imposter syndrome is a common experience that can affect anyone, regardless of their level of success or expertise. It is important to recognize and address these feelings by acknowledging your achievements, seeking support from others, and reframing negative self-perceptions. Remember, you have valuable skills and abilities that deserve recognition.

Code Switching

Code switching refers to the practice of altering one's language, dialect, or communication style based on the social context or audience.

I called my friend at work and asked to speak to her, not knowing or recognizing her voice when she answered the phone. The operator or secretary answering the call did put the call through correctly. However, the receiver's voice was unfamiliar to me.

I would apologize by saying "I'm sorry, I was trying to reach..." and say her name. I would then hear a chuckle or laugh, and she would say in a voice, tone, and diction that I recognized "Girrrl dis me." This is not a new concept for me. I just did not know the technical term. I recall growing up hearing people speak "proper" on the phone to disguise their voices from bill collectors.

Code switching is a form of masking that, although it has purpose, hides our authentic selves. It can be used for cultural adaptation which allows individuals to navigate different cultural environments and adapt their communication-style to fit in or be better understood.

It is used as a form of social acceptance to gain approval from a particular social group or community and foster a sense of belonging. I have experienced it primarily in professional or academic settings to conform to the language and communication norms of those environments. It can enhance credibility and facilitate effective communication.

Filtering

Filtering what you say, or your response means to carefully consider and choose your words or actions before expressing them. It involves being mindful of the impact your words may have on others and making conscious decisions about what information or opinions to share. It is also a method used to manage your emotions.

Filtering allows you to consider the context, audience, and potential consequences of your words. In other words, there are somethings that you can say in a setting with close personal friends that you wouldn't necessarily say in a professional setting. By filtering, you can ensure that your response is appropriate, respectful, and considerate of others' feelings and perspectives.

When you filter your message and-or response this involves practicing self-control and thoughtfulness. You purposefully refrain from sharing certain information that could be hurtful or sensitive, avoiding offensive or inappropriate language, or choosing a more diplomatic and tactful approach when expressing your thoughts and-or opinions. It promotes effective communication, positive relationships, and avoids unnecessary conflicts or misunderstandings.

Most importantly, it demonstrates respect, empathy, and emotional intelligence.

As it relates to emotional wellness, filtering allows you to pause and reflect before speaking, giving you the opportunity to consider the potential impact of your words so you can avoid saying something hurtful or regrettable in the heat of the moment. When we respond from our feelings, our judgment can be clouded, and this can lead to impulsive or irrational responses.

Filtering your words leads to clearer, more respectful, and constructive conversations that will help avoid misunderstandings and promote healthier communication with others. Furthermore, filtering can have a positive impact on thinking patterns. This process helps you to shape your internal thoughts and emotions in a more positive and constructive way.

However, let me make a clear distinction here, filtering what you say should not be confused with suppressing or denying your emotions. Meaning do not mask them! To properly manage your emotions and maintain emotional wellness it is essential that you acknowledge and validate your emotions. It is also important to find a balance between filtering and expressing your emotions, and the transforming-your-reality-removing-the-mask tools will help you achieve this. It is imperative to be open and honest in your communications because this is crucial for healthy relationships and personal growth.

Masking a Learned Behavior

Innate. children enter this world as a blank slate to be shaped and molded by the family in which they are born. They learn through observation and the images that are being modeled by people in the world that they have access to. As infants, the behavior of the adults in their environment is a reaction to the child's level of comfort and is often an ongoing attempt to keep a baby happy, pleased, and calm. As the child moves through developmental stages, what is seen as negative behavior is frowned upon by their parents and the larger society.

Just think about that crying child in church, or on the plane. The child who hits, or bites, or just won't cooperate. These children hear the phases, no, stop that, that is bad, we don't tolerate that kind of behavior in this house, etc. When children are sad, we instantly try to cheer them up and try to make them happy again. Little effort is given to why they are sad, angry, upset, or afraid. These emotions are ignored, and the child soon realizes, or thinks, that I am supposed to be happy all the time. That is what is acceptable and pleasing to my parents and others around me.

Culture. It has a strong influence on how we behave, our values and beliefs, the choices we make, and how we see ourselves in comparison to others in society. It is hardwired and passed down from generation to generation. It provides us with guidelines and parameters that can restrict, prohibit, or empower our ability to act in what is deemed appropriate as it relates to our upbringing, norms, and pre-scripted behavior. Some people don't know why they like or dislike people, places, or things. They usually say, "that's just how I am." They are not cognizant of the fact that their dislike could be a part of the scripted behavior that they have witnessed in their family for years.

Societal Influence

Unfortunately, we live in a society where comparison is the norm. When comparing is the norm, it will be difficult to find true happiness. In fact, everything we say or do is under a microscope. This is the overarching premise behind "Cancel Culture." Is this holding people accountable to ensure that they align actions with words? Is this punishment for not agreeing with society's majority, leaving a group or person out, sharing one's true feelings and thoughts, being insensitive, or perhaps, rushing to take a stand or statement without having all of the facts? There's so much controversy about every public thought and opinion that organizations, managers, publicists, and branding and marketing specialists have to sensor every move an organization makes and words that are uttered that can make, break, and-or ruin images overnight.

False Imaging. The cosmetic and beauty industry brings in billions yearly. Even during the COVID-19 pandemic when for the most part we were isolated in our homes, this industry remained lucrative. We are very visual beings. Appearance is the first level of acceptance. As a people we are attracted to beauty. If we think we are unappealing we will mask any imperfection by make-up, to give the illusion of having confidence, charisma, and intelligence. We are like magicians constantly deflecting and keeping others from seeing what's really happening. Unfortunately, sometimes we become part of the illusion.

Contortion of your true identity is a crime against all that you were created to be. We are not cookie cutter images of what is acceptable in our society. God made us each unique. Our fingerprints and voice patterns don't match anyone else's on this planet and there are other distinguishable markers as well. It becomes a crime when we steal images from what is deemed acceptable and layer them over who we really are or what God made when He created us.

Being different has become more readily accepted, or let's say tolerated, in the 21st century. However, difference has in some cases taken on an unpredictable look under the guise or pretense of polar-opposites. Self-expression is very colorful as it ranges from gothic to rainbow hair, an array of outfits, body piercings and coloring, and styles that can also be a form of masking by helping us hide the pain of emotions that bombard us daily as we continue to veer from our authentic selves.

This is an indicator that masking encompasses people of all ages from middle school and up. It is reinforced by the groups we connect with and-or accept us. It's part of the secret search to find who we really are and reconnect with our authentic selves.

I will conclude this chapter by stating that masking has no one to blame. There are many factors that lead to this phenomenon. However, it is important to approach this topic with sensitivity and recognize that individual experiences may differ. We have examined common factors that contribute to why people mask their feelings and emotions.

There are several influences to include societal and expectations of others, culture, upbringing, fear of judgment or rejection, past and present traumas, and a lack of emotional awareness or coping skills. There could possibly be many combinations of factors that create barriers that keep us from expressing emotions openly and authentically.

Use these tools *(your workbook & companion journal)* provided to foster an environment where you feel safe to express your emotions without fear of judgment or rejection. Then, use this book to encourage emotional literacy, as a resource for emotional well-being, and to help create a space where you feel comfortable enough to be authentic with your feelings and emotions.

Facing Your Reality

I'll start this chapter with a literary piece that was written by an African American poet, Paul Laurence Dunbar. He wrote this poem in 1896 as part of a collection of poems titled *Lyrics of a Lowly Life*. Dunbar illustrates the true reality underneath the mask we wear while painting an all too familiar picture of what others see.

WE WEAR THE MASK

We wear the mask that grins and lies,

It hides our cheeks and shades our eyes,—

This debt we pay to human guile;

With torn and bleeding hearts we smile,

And mouth with myriad subtleties.

Why should the world be over-wise,

In counting all our tears and sighs?

Nay, let them only see us, while

We wear the mask.

We smile, but, O great Christ, our cries

To thee from tortured souls arise.

We sing, but oh the clay is vile

Beneath our feet, and long the mile;

But let the world dream otherwise,

We wear the mask!

Since we mask it becomes hard for us to remember, identify, and face the truth. This can be a very difficult process and yet, a turning point in people's lives. The brain is a very complicated and intricate organ. Its functions are divided into regions that connect through neurotransmitters. Each component of the brain houses our intelligence, thoughts, memories, perceptions, and controls our bodily functions.

However, the brain in all its amazement can be tricked and will believe whatever it perceives to be true even when it is not true. The key word here is perceiving. Belief can be based on what you see through your eyes, in daytime and nightly dreams, and in your thoughts. Perception is influenced by a persons' beliefs, morals, values, experiences, culture, and environment.

For many, our environments are shaped by social media in some form or fashion, and we are constantly bombarded by images, social pressures, and perceived norms and defects that can make or break social mobility, social acceptance, social status, and more. For these reasons and more, we MASK! The mask, although invisible, is perceived as a layer of protection. It hides what we consider flawed, broken, damaged, and imperfect. Things in our past or future that we don't want others to see or know about.

Whatever the situation, in our attempt to cover it we also feel the emotions that accompany that action, event, situation, lie, or trauma and we cover those emotions as well. The bible teaches us that the truth shall set you free and this statement is the emphasis of this chapter.

Often what we are covering with our mask has been concealed for many years. We may now be fathers, mothers, CEOs, lawyers, and outwardly very successful. Although we have grown and matured beyond what we are hiding, emotionally we are stuck at the point where the suffering began. The abandonment, betrayal, grief, hurt, neglect and whatever has traumatized you is where the real you still resides emotionally.

This became evident as I worked with families in the community. There were people whose mask had them playing the role of Dr. Jekyll and Mr. Hide. There were times when they began to break from the strain of masking day-in and day-out; that their authentic self would show-up and their true reality was instantly bombarded by an unforgiving world, accusing thoughts, and immediately of being ostracized by those who perceived the real you as different; that it was easier to retreat behind the mask and endure the pain of masking.

Mental health in the U.S. has made tremendous strides, but we still have a way to go. Advocacy programs bring awareness and provide education, but many are apprehensive about asking for, or receiving, support. Some of my clients became frustrated with the process. They wanted to remove layers of emotions that have been hidden for years in just a few visits. This frustration is fueled by the cost of treatment, the inability to get timely appointments, insurance caps, and timeframes *(6-8 visits)* that are placed on mental health treatment.

Most importantly, the stigma still exists. People do not want their employers, family members, spouses, or even children to know that they are seeking treatment. They suffer in silence and seek help in silence too. Mental health fits right in with masking because in many cases you can't see it until the person has reached their breaking point requiring a residential treatment facility, hospitalization either on an inpatient psychiatric unit or at a psychiatric hospital, or rehabilitation centers.

I remember one of my clients asking what is real. She shared that she had masked as a child because she wanted to be "the good one" *(child)*. She masked at school because she wanted to please her parents and teachers -- she wanted to be "the good one"*(student)*. She never wanted to cause anyone else any strife; people could always count on her to be "the good one." Even at work she strived to be that person who did above and beyond regardless of how people treated her because she wanted to be "the good one."

She told me that parenthood was difficult for her, and she even thought that she suffered from postpartum depression after giving birth to her children, but she didn't complain or seek help because she wanted to be seen as "the good one" *(wife, mother)*. This pattern has existed for so long in her life that she believed her true authentic self to be this weak shell of a person racked with fear and shame due to her inability to stand up and be herself. She knew in her heart of hearts that God had created her to be a masterpiece; since she felt she wasn't, she thought God was disappointed in her too.

Facing reality is difficult for some to conceive because we live in a dichotomous reality. There has always been a struggle between good and evil since Adam and Eve. I remember as a child watching a cartoon show where the character was continuously faced with situations that made him choose; to illustrate this moment, a devil and an angel would appear opposite sides on each shoulder. Even as a child it seems the devils' choices were easier *(acting on emotions)* than the angels' choices *(acting on reason)*. In the church they speak of living in the flesh and living in the spirit.

We are emotional beings; those who are ruled by their emotions are labeled risk takers, out of control, carefree; however, those guided by reason are seen as rigid, inflexible, and dogmatic. In many of us it is a combination of them both. The truth of the matter is, we all fall short of perfection. Instead of embracing reality, we paint the illusion of contentment, flawlessness, and happiness on the mask that we adorn to ensure our acceptance by family, friends, co-workers, and society.

When we mask, we lower the bar that has been set by our creator. We disrupt his plan which is uniquely designed with the gifts and talents that are housed in each of us. This is why many people are said to be experiencing a mid-life crisis. They want to purge and-or uncover their gifts and talents. They no longer feel pressured to live out others' dreams or desires for their life.

Most importantly, they are exhausted from, and no longer want, to settle for the pretense of happiness. They are in search of what truly makes them happy as some feel that they have more years behind them than they have in front of them. In the words of Jill Scotts lyrics from her song Golden:

I'm holding on to my freedom
Can't take it from me
I was born into it
It comes naturally
I'm strumming my own freedom
Playing the God in me
Representing his glory
Hope he's proud of me

I'm livin' my life like it's golden

Part of the struggle we experience when we mask is due to working to achieve in an area outside of our giftings. I remember when my children were younger, as parents, my husband and I wanted to help them discover their gifts, talents, and purpose. We had both read Ken Robinson's book *The Element: How Finding Your Passion Changes Everything*, and we vowed to help our children find theirs.

So, we immersed them in a plethora of clubs, activities, and sports. It became obvious what their true gifts and talents were and were not. We helped them explore their interest and discovered they had many talents, so we let them enjoy operating in their giftings. My 6'2" son was never forced to play sports even though he had the build for it, agility, and speed, and had a family history in track and football.

Every time someone saw him, they immediately assumed he was athletic. We would always change the subject to talk about his writing, academics, and other areas that he excelled in. We immersed him in activities so he could continue to strengthen his true gifts and grow and develop.

I was glad to see my children soar but felt as if I was standing in quicksand. I could remember feeling that there was something more, or else, that I should be doing and felt empty at times. Oh, I had a beautiful life but just felt as if I kept missing the mark. Questioning am I a good mother, sister, daughter, wife, and friend. I wore many hats in the community and wondered if I was falling short in one of those areas.

Like many, I overcompensated trying to be all things to everybody except me, and even feeling guilty when I did do something for myself. I felt like a hamster on a wheel. The harder I worked, the faster I moved in circles. During this period, I looked happy, and I was happy for everyone else but me. As parents we tend to build up our children, our legacy, our future, and place our dreams on the back burner.

This is a delicate area, because in the field of mental health, I have worked with families that struggle with parent-child relationships. The parents were so busy building a better life based on income that they failed to build-up their children. Some were career-focused, self-absorbed, dealing with issues from their childhood, detached, and some had not completed the courses and handbook on "How to Be a Parent" that automatically comes long before the baby. For those who did not have good, or any, role model, or who were reared during an era when children had to survive versus succeed and thrive, they emulated what they had seen or learned from others, mixed with guesswork. This chapter is very important, so before I move on let me recap:

When you take off that mask you see the power and hand of God at work in your life and His love will be able to reach your heart igniting happiness, peace, and love from within....no mask necessary.

So, keep these steps in mind as you move toward the process of facing reality:

1. **UNDERSTAND** that life is precious and don't waste time pursuing other's dreams.
2. **TAKE PRIDE** in who God created and don't be afraid to show that person to the world.
3. **DISCOVER** your gifts, Proverbs 18:16(NKJV) includes a powerful statement about the gift or talent in every person. This is your core design: "A man's gift makes room for him."

Thought Change

What we believe is reinforced by our thoughts. As humans we tend to gravitate towards negative thoughts especially in the highly critical society that we live in. It is like we are trained to detect flaws and the moment one is detected the floodgates of criticism, cynicism, and accusations are opened. Why does this occur?

Well, information that is true is easily dismissed because it does not always elicit the same emotional response as negative information, and this makes it easier to dismiss or overlook. Let's think about it this way. When we mask our insecurities, flaws, the things we worry, feel ashamed, or guilty about as well as numerous other hurtful, tragic, and traumatic events, those thoughts don't go anywhere. It might be easier for us to ignore them when they are masked but those negative thoughts feed our minds and what you feed grows! This is why it is so easy to think the worst.

A friend of mine recently passed the bar exam. She was ecstatic and I was so happy for her. Later that evening her family and friends met at a restaurant to celebrate her achievements. One of the women sitting beside me leaned over to another member of the group and said, "You know she took the exam three times before she passed it and just barely passed the third time."

A flaw had been detected and immediately there was an attempt to diminish her accomplishments, to sabotage my friend's victory. I leaned over, introduced myself and asked *do you have a law degree, what law firm do you work for?*

It is quite easy to plant a seed of doubt. We will believe negative information without any hesitation, thought or investigation. However, belief on the other hand must be confirmed, affirmed, solidified, sources checked, and documents reviewed. This type of thinking helps to perpetuate the mask.

By burying any and all flaws, people do not have to deal with negativity bias -- this is the natural inclination to pay more attention to negative information as a survival mechanism. It is a way to identify potential threats and dangers to our environment. Who wants to be connected to someone who has done something negative that could possibly impact you?

It is easier for negative information or lies to align with preconceived notions or negative expectations. This can happen often when one piece of negative information is used to connect with an incident that happened in a person's family years ago. Most importantly, negative information can evoke strong emotional responses, such as fear, anger, or sadness. These emotions can cloud judgment and make it more difficult to critically evaluate the information.

How does our environment influence our thinking? This is a theory that I have had the opportunity to explore from a qualitative research perspective.

My husband and I have been married for 34 years. He is an avid reader and working primarily in the automotive sales industry. He has listened to tapes of motivational speakers, attended trainings, viewed podcast, and read books by numerous authors on self-development, sales, leadership, and positive thinking. I know as a university professor you think that surely, I too have read numerous books, but I must admit that as it relates to motivation and leadership, I am a vicarious learner.

I have not studied these concepts but instead, gleaned information from my husband's discussion of the materials and being in the car and listening to tapes and recordings of various speakers. My children and I heard a multitude of inspirational messages during our long-distance 14-hour trips from Alabama to Virginia as we traveled home as a family about every 4-5 months to see my parents. These messages permeated our conscious and subconscious thoughts.

I now believe that even as my children slept during our travels that they unconsciously absorbed the messages. As a result, every member in the family by osmoses became wired for success and are very successful. But before you load your children in the car and start playing motivational and inspirational recordings and podcasts, I must warn you that this type of thinking can have perks as well as drawbacks.

Drawback: My children are very task-oriented and work off a daily plan. This can limit room for spontaneity and exploration, and even task or goal incompletion. It can also stifle creativity.

Reality Check: It's okay if you don't finish first, or in the top 10. It's okay if you don't finish or reach your goal. Life won't end. Sometimes things don't work out so don't be afraid. Face that truth and try it anyway. Failure is a reality. It's important to remember that the lessons from failure breed success.

Drawback: I can remember getting a solemn phone call from my son when he was a sophomore in college. He thought that he'd failed a course that would determine if he would get into the engineering program at Virginia Tech. He asked me would I still be proud of him if he was not an engineer.

Reality Check: That question cut me like a knife. I thought, how could he think that? Had I said something, or did something, to make him feel that being an engineer would impact the pride and love that I have for him? Does he not know that I am so very proud and love him because he is my son? How could he confuse my love with a course, degree, college, or title? Did he think my pride was superficial and my love conditional?! Maybe he was looking at me from the mask that I wore *(for others)* to hide my insecurities and vulnerabilities. The mask *(obstruction)* kept him from seeing his mom as her authentic, transparent self.

Benefits: Some of the positive take-aways are that each of my children possess laser-sharp focus. The Lord only knows where I would be today if at their age, I had that type of focus. In addition, they do not get caught up in what is popular, or having the latest fashion, or chasing trends or other people's dreams. With the exception of sports, they do not watch television and believe in free expression through books, podcasts, editing, speaking, and a host of other gifts and talents.

Stinking Thinking

Motivational messages that inspire change through trainings, studying, and working to uncover the God given gifts and talents that are within you and come from the Creator, I can support, but we also need to address the turmoil of negative emotions that you have masked. So, what others see is not a partial façade.

I do believe in positive thinking and looking for the good in every situation, but this is not the same as smiling, being cheerful, or forcing positivity when that is not how I truly feel. I have met people who have changed their lives and achieved great things as leaders in their prospective fields with the help of motivational messages and leadership books. But they still wear masks; they struggle with pain, heart-ache, and loss like everyone else.

Author Napoleon Hill introduces the concept of Positive Mental Attitude (PMA) in his self-help book in 1937, *Think And Grow Rich*. The moral of his mes-sage is to approach every situation and challenge in life with optimism. He explains that the right mind-set attracts positive circumstances and includes suc-cess, health, and happiness. The pressure to be happy is reinforced in many popular songs "Put On A Happy Face," "Don't Worry Be Happy," "Happy Peo-ple," "Happy" and many other hits suggest that we exalt happiness, but it sometimes comes at the cost of hiding and-or ignoring our true feelings.

The philosophy behind PMA suggests that it pos-itively impacts behavior and emotions, hope, opti-mism, courage, and kindness. Practicing PMA means not giving into negative energy or feelings of hope-lessness even in difficult situations. In my opinion, this aligns with toxic positivity; finding good in every situation when in reality there is nothing good about tragedy, trauma, and grief.

During COVID-19 millions lost their lives, the world as we knew it changed forever. As a person who lived through the pandemic you feel the loss, hurt, pain, suffering, anger and a variation of emotions and feelings that cannot be addressed by thinking positively and having a positive attitude alone. I am reminded of the song title by CeCe and BeBe Winans "Millions Didn't Make It." The lyrics continue with, "but I was one of the ones who did", although this song talks about a life with Jesus, I connect it to those who were lost during the pandemic and that feels and looks different for everybody.

To tell someone to not give into how they are feeling is dangerous and forces them to put on the mask to hide any feelings that would be considered an outlier based on this philosophy and the overall pressure by society to be and achieve happiness. I am sure that the philosophy behind PMA is fluid and has been updated since 1937 and does consider extenuating circumstances, but people's thinking can be rigid.

Even as it relates to thinking positive, a dichotomous reality exists. Thinking positive is a good thing as it relates to worry, doubt, and being hopeful. However, in other situations, positive thinking quickly turns into faulty thinking because no amount of positivity can negate experiences such as rape, neglect, abuse, and a host of other tragic outcomes.

Faulty thinking can cloud our judgment and keep us from seeing what is happening. Faulty thinking can lead to falsely accusing others and placing blame, inability to take accountability or responsibility, and being a perpetual victim. Because this type of thinking usually makes circumstances worse, people can sometimes feel powerless and lose hope. Some situations are just bad and what you are truly feeling needs to be taken into consideration, dealt with, and not masked.

I was at an event for women of domestic violence, and I heard words like overcomer and survivor showered over many of the victims; undoubtedly, they are; although they are no longer in an abusive relationship, people must realize that the psychological and physical trauma associated with the abuse is deep-seated.

Thinking positive does not touch the surface of emotions associated with this level of violence and-or threats of violence. The problem occurs when people who have experienced traumatic and PTSD situations believe that having positive mental attitude *(PMA)* is all they need to heal and overcome their situations and that it is also where recovery begins and ends. In this situation, the mask can become a vital part of survival.

Understand, I am not saying that you should let negative emotions and uncertainty dictate your daily thoughts and actions. What I am saying is that negative emotions, feelings, and experiences will not go away just because you exchanged them for positive happy thoughts. There will be triggers, situations, and antecedents that make you feel and relive that trauma repeatedly. In addition, it is easy to tuck emotional trauma underneath a mask. Unlike a physical injury, emotional trauma is not visible, and its effects are difficult for the individual to detect. It becomes normalized.

However, when left unresolved it never heals and remnants of the pain will begin to show up in relationships or interactions with others and self. This brokenness can turn inward and-or outward. Inwardly drugs and alcohol are used in an attempt to soothe the discomfort or feel better. Many of the children that I have worked with who came from abusive situations had parents whose trauma could be traced back for generations. Outwardly brokenness can manifest in various ways, but generally, it refers to individuals who have experienced personal struggles or hardships and project their pain onto others.

In both adults and children this can result in behaviors such as aggression, hostility, manipulation, or even cruelty towards others. They can struggle with empathy and often find it difficult to form healthy relationships. Because broken people tear down others *(critical and always finding fault)* instead of building them up or looking for strengths, they may not know what a healthy relationship looks like. The workbook approaches brokenness with understanding and compassion, to help uncover and address the root causes to help promote healing and personal growth.

Reality Check

Personally, I try to keep a positive attitude and give most people the benefit of the doubt. I think this was first ingrained in me during my undergraduate social work program. The focus was on strength building, meeting the person in their environment, being open and respectful of others' views, beliefs, and values. However, the authentic me understands that once that reality has been challenged it becomes more difficult to fake positivity.

People will disappoint you. I recall the famous quote by Maya Angelou, "When someone shows you who they are, believe them the first time."

As human beings we harbor a multitude of feelings and not all of them are positive. There will not always be a bright side to every situation. The truth of the matter is that we don't always feel positive. Even when tragic things happen in our lives people will remind us of the bright side. Well-meaning people use toxic positivity to respond to your traumatic situations with false hope. Reassuring you that "time heals all wounds", "your loved one doesn't have to suffer anymore."

This may be true, but it does not negate the pain, suffering, devastation, and all the other phases we experience as we move through, in and out, or get stuck in Elizabeth Kubler Ross' stages of grief. These feelings can permeate our very soul; however, the push by family and friends is to "stay away from" *(ignore)* the dark places in your mind and run to the light -- the happy place that has been painted by the delusional brush strokes of joyful images that are adorned by others around us and reinforced by society.

I've mentioned this concept of positive toxicity, or toxic positivity *(they are used synonymously)* a few times throughout this chapter to drive home the importance of understanding what it is, and how to identify it as this is vital during your unmasking process.

Trauma

Whenever I am presenting the topic of unmasking, I always assess the audience to see how many people have experienced trauma. When they hear the question, they automatically think about physical abuse or neglect and respond to the question based on that premise. However, there are many types of traumas, but for the purpose of this section, I will focus on the not-so-obvious, *vicarious trauma*. From this lens, it is clear to see that in some aspects of our lives we have all been traumatized. The biggest culprit today is this type of second-hand trauma.

As a mental health provider, I am keenly aware of the transference that occurs when I take on a case and work with children and families who have experienced some form or multiple forms of trauma. There is a transference of culpability between the direct service provider and the client. Providers experience the emotional baggage that engulfs the situation as well as the responsibility they have to their agency, and everyone involved including their client.

In fact, vicarious trauma sneaks up on all of us when we watch the news witnessing war, violence, death, suicide, and other gut-wrenching events. Social media helps to ensure that the trauma is constant and provides us with access to events around the world. But most unexpectantly, it occurs as we listen as someone else's family member, friend, acquaintances, neighbors share their stories of pain and heartache. We are wired that way and whether we show it or not, we feel others pain and sometimes deeply.

I was interviewed on a show that addressed school bullying, and vicarious trauma reigned. The parents of the children who were bullied experienced in some cases more emotional turmoil over their child being bullied than the children did. They took on the extra persona of blame, fault, shame, and helplessness. The tears would well up in their eyes as they relived events second-hand and the mask and walls that they had created to hide the pain of the situation briefly fell behind the pressures of truth and transparency.

Effects of Faulty Thinking

Many people mask so that they can carry out the realities that match the images they portray to the world. Maintaining the mask is a complex process. Proverbs 23:7(KJV) For as he **thinketh** within himself, **so is he**. Key word here is thinketh! When we mask, we start down the rabbit hole of faulty thinking. This is a common cognitive error, and we all do it. In your mind and sometimes out loud you will say, "What was I thinking?!"

This type of altered perception occurs when our thought patterns don't match up with reality. Bishop T. D. Jake's book _Disruptive Thinking_ illustrates the concept of faulty thinking and how one must unmask faulty thoughts to achieve eruption of thought. When thoughts erupt, individuals free themselves from an unhealthy belief system so they can see through the lens of transparency long enough to face reality and find truth. John 8:32 "Then you will know the truth, and the truth will set you free." In other words, masking hides the truth and keeps you in bondage.

Whenever you hide the truth, you hide the most authentic part of yourself: the part that God made when He created you. Unmasking is necessary because the stress of maintaining an alternative reality day-in and day-out affects our mental health *(mind)* and permeates our body and soul. The statement health providers make about how stress kills is so true! We know how it impacts the body by interrupting normal functions and systems that support the heart, blood pressure, insulin regulation, immune system, lungs, and cell formation.

Stress can be linked with chronic illness and end-stage diseases. However, we seldom think about how it impacts our soul and spirit. High levels of stress mixed with faulty thinking can be toxic. People can become so depleted of hope until death *(suicide)* becomes a viable option.

You don't know how to manage your emotions, and this is not your fault! You have never been taught how, or allowed to share, your true feelings for fear of seeming weak, fear that you might become or feel out-of-control, and not wanting others to think something is wrong with you. You employ tactics like faulty thinking/cognitive distortions, toxic positivity, and ancestral guilt, that suggest we should just "deal with it."

You have been conditioned to manage your emotions and feelings by minimizing, excuses, ignoring, blaming others, jumping to conclusions, overgeneralizations, not taking responsibility, defensiveness, and by utilizing techniques *(that I share throughout the workbook)* to protect your psyche. You will accept advice from people who are not trained experts in the field but seeking professional help.

We've covered a lot in this chapter -- this is a good place to reinforce what has been shared with an activity.

Release Activity *(you need the companion journal and workbook for this)*

Use the companion journal to release the feelings and emotions associated with the trauma that you have experienced. If you feel like you need additional support in this area, use the appendix in the back of any of the Transforming Your Reality Removing the Mask books/tools to access additional resources.

Activity-6: Use information from this chapter along with Activity (6) workbook and the companion journal as needed to gain deeper personal insight in this area.

Discovering Emotional Wellness

FIGHT OR FLIGHT

When we bury trauma of any type it forces us to stay in "fight or flight" mode, where your brain stays on high alert; prepared for dangerous situations 24/7. Operating in a constant state of "fight or flight" mode, also known as chronic stress, can have significant effects on both physical and mental well-being. Here are some potential consequences:

Physical health: Prolonged activation of the stress response can lead to various physical health issues. It can weaken the immune system, making individuals more susceptible to illnesses and infections. Chronic stress has also been linked to cardiovascular problems, high blood pressure, digestive issues, headaches, and sleep disturbances.

Mental health: Continuous activation of the stress response can contribute to the development or exacerbation of mental health conditions. It may increase the risk of anxiety disorders, depression, and burnout. Chronic stress can also impair cognitive function, memory, and concentration.

Emotional wellness: Living in a constant state of fight or flight can lead to heightened emotional reactivity and difficulty regulating emotions. Individuals may experience irritability, anger, frustration, and a reduced ability to cope with everyday stressors. It can also impact relationships and social interactions.

One way to keep our brains out of continuous fight or flight mode is by practicing emotional wellness. Emotional wellness is not a one and done concept. It is an ongoing process that requires self-reflection, self-care, and continuous growth. It plays a crucial role in overall well-being and can positively impact various aspects of life, including relationships, work, and personal fulfillment.

EMOTIONAL WELLNESS

Emotional wellness is the transformation once the mask is removed and the emotions that we have buried for years are addressed and managed. Emotional wellness refers to the state of being aware and accepting of one's emotions, effectively managing them, and maintaining a positive overall emotional state. It involves understanding and expressing emotions in a healthy and constructive manner, as well as developing resilience to cope with life's challenges.

As it pertains to understanding; my question here is where do we learn how to effectively manage our emotions? Who teaches us? Is learning how to manage emotions taught in any of our k-12 curriculums?

I just don't remember my parents, or anybody saying, "today we are going to talk about the 6-15- 30 *(this number varies based on psychologist and researchers)* basic emotions you will experience, and this is how you manage each one." This was not a topic brought up at the dinner table, during the holidays, or on the playground with my friends, etc. This is of no fault to my parents, or your parents, or their parents, or generations before them.

However, Social Emotional Learning programs are being used in some states, and to what degree varies according to a survey conducted by the Collaborative for Academic Social and Emotional Learning in 2022-2023. These programs are designed to help students develop self-awareness, self-management, social-management, social awareness, relationship skills, and responsible decision making.

It is great that some efforts are being implemented to help address emotional wellness with school-aged youth. However, the truth is that the concept of emotions is so complex that it really takes a mental health professional, such as a psychiatrist, psychologist, licensed therapist, or counselor *(someone who is qualified)* to teach people how to manage their emotions effectively. These professionals have years of specialized training and are experts in understanding and addressing emotional challenges.

Throughout my workbook I encourage users to seek professional guidance and support from specialists who use evidence-based techniques to help individuals develop healthy coping mechanisms and emotional regulation skills.

According to psychologist Paul Ekman, there are six basic emotions:

Happiness: Feeling joy, contentment, or pleasure.

Sadness: Experiencing feelings of sorrow, grief, or unhappiness.

Anger: Feeling frustration, annoyance, or hostility.

Fear: Experiencing anxiety, apprehension, or terror.

Disgust: Feeling revulsion, aversion, or repulsion.

Surprise: Experiencing astonishment, amazement, or unexpectedness.

It's important to note that these basic emotions can combine and interact with each other, leading to a wide range of complex emotional experiences. Additionally, some researchers propose the inclusion of other emotions like love, shame, guilt, and more as basic emotions. The understanding of emotions is a complex and evolving field of study, and different theories may offer different perspectives on the number and nature of basic emotions.

Within the field of mental health and in my work with children, adolescents, and their families. I learned the term comorbidity. Because emotions are so complex, I believe that comorbidity can exist in relation to emotions.

Comorbidity refers to the presence of two, or more, medical, or psychiatric conditions occurring in the same individual simultaneously. In the context of emotions, comorbidity would be the co-occurrence of multiple emotional disorders, or conditions. I saw this often in clients with mood disorders, substance abuse issues, and post-traumatic stress.

In my workbook I ask readers to complete a few assessment tools, such as, *The Holmes and Rahe Stress Scale: A Self-Assessment to Understand the Impact of Long-Term Stress, Life Stressor Checklist,* and *Five Stages of Grief Wellness Index.* In doing so, it can provide a greater understanding of their emotional state and the possible need for professional help from mental health practitioners who can provide an accurate diagnosis and develop an appropriate treatment plan that meets their individual and unique needs.

It is important to note that achieving and maintaining emotional wellness is the key to a better life, discovering your authentic-self and living the life that God planned for you. Our emotions connect every aspect of our bodies and has a profound effect on our overall health.

When we mask our emotions, we tend to think that everything else will function normally. On the contrary, masking emotions negatively impacts the entire body. Mental and emotional stress can manifest as negative physical reactions, negative emotional reactions, and a weakened immune system. The six key aspects of emotional wellness include:

Self-awareness: Being in tune with your emotions, recognizing and understanding them, and being aware of how they impact your thoughts, behaviors, and overall well-being.

Emotional regulation: Developing healthy coping mechanisms and strategies to manage and regulate emotions, such as stress, anger, sadness, or anxiety. This involves finding healthy outlets for emotions and avoiding harmful or destructive behaviors.

Emotional intelligence: Having the ability to recognize and understand emotions in oneself and others, and effectively navigate social interactions and relationships. This includes empathy, active listening, and effective communication skills.

Resilience: Building the capacity to bounce back from setbacks, adapt to change, and effectively cope with stress and adversity. It involves developing healthy coping mechanisms, seeking support when needed, and maintaining a positive outlook.

Self-care: Prioritizing and engaging in activities that promote emotional well-being, such as practicing self-compassion, engaging in hobbies, maintaining healthy relationships, and taking time for relaxation and self-reflection.

Seeking support: Recognizing when additional support is needed and seeking help from trusted in-dividuals, such as friends, family, or mental health professionals. This can include therapy, counseling, or support groups.

I've included some tips below to help you create a state of peace as you unmask and begin to address and manage previously masked emotions.

CREATING A STATE OF PEACE

This can be as simple as taking a breath!

Breathing is a fundamental and essential aspect of creating personal peace. We know that oxygen nourishes our mind, body, and soul and without it we die, but there's more to it than that. Here's how breathing can help us find our peace:

Stress reduction: Deep, intentional breathing activates the body's relaxation response, which helps to counteract the effects of stress. It triggers the parasympathetic nervous system, promoting a state of calmness and relaxation.

Mind-body connection: Focusing on your breath brings your attention to the present moment and helps you connect with your body. This mindfulness practice can help you become more aware of your thoughts, emotions, and physical sensations, allowing you to cultivate a sense of inner peace and self-awareness.

Emotional regulation: Breathing techniques, such as deep-belly breathing or diaphragmatic breathing, can help regulate emotions by activating the body's relaxation response. This can be particularly helpful in managing feelings of anxiety, anger, or being overwhelmed, allowing you to find a sense of peace amidst challenging emotions.

Increased clarity and focus: Deep, conscious breathing can help clear the mind and improve focus. By bringing oxygen to the brain, it enhances cognitive function, concentration, and mental clarity. This can create a sense of peace by reducing mental clutter and promoting a state of centeredness.

Finding Your Body Rhythm

This is also known as establishing a regular routine, or rhythm, in your daily life. I know that in this fast-paced world we live in, the playing field is always changing, and we are constantly adjusting just so that we can keep up with what seems impossible to do. Know that it is a vital step in creating and finding your peace for several reasons:

Improved physical health: Having a consistent body rhythm helps regulate your sleep patterns, digestion, and metabolism. It allows your body to function optimally, leading to better overall physical health.

Enhanced mental well-being: Establishing a body rhythm can contribute to better mental health by reducing stress, anxiety, and mood swings. It provides a sense of stability and predictability, which can promote feelings of calmness and control.

Increased productivity: When you have a consistent body rhythm, your body and mind become accustomed to certain activities at specific times. This can enhance your productivity and efficiency as you will be more equipped to focus and concentrate on tasks.

Improved sleep quality: Maintaining a regular sleep schedule and bedtime routine helps regulate your body's internal clock, known as the circadian rhythm. This can lead to better sleep quality, increased energy levels, and improved cognitive function during the day.

Better time management: Establishing a body rhythm helps you prioritize and allocate time for different activities, such as work, exercise, relaxation, and socializing. This can help you manage your time more effectively and achieve a better work-life balance.

Enhanced overall well-being: Having a consistent body rhythm promotes a sense of stability, routine, and balance in your life. It can contribute to a greater sense of overall well-being, satisfaction, and happiness.

Recognize and Utilize Your Coping Skills

Coping skills are strategies or techniques that individuals can use to manage and deal with stress, emotions, and-or difficult situations. There are a few steps here:

- First identify the skills that you are currently using.
    - o Start by making a list of your current coping skills and how effective or ineffective they are. To answer this ask yourself the following:

- Do the coping skills that I am using help to relieve the intense feelings or emotions being experienced?
- Am I just ignoring or masking the feelings?
- Am I just pretending and-or telling myself and others that I am, okay?

If the coping skills you use are not relieving the intense feelings or emotions you may be feeling, replace them with one or more of the strategies below:

- Deep breathing exercises.
- Mindfulness and meditation.
- Engage in physical activity, or exercise.
- Practice relaxation techniques, such as progressive muscle relaxation.
- Journal, or write down thoughts and feelings.
- Seek support from friends, family, or a support group.
- Engage in hobbies or activities that bring joy or relaxation.
- Set and maintain healthy boundaries.
- Practice self-care activities, such as taking a bath or getting a massage.
- Use positive self-talk and affirmations.
- Engage in creative outlets, such as art or music.
- Seek professional help, or therapy.

- Take breaks and practice self-compassion.
- Set realistic goals and prioritize tasks.
- Avoid, or manage, triggers and stressful situations.

Remember, coping skills can vary from person-to-person, so it's important to find what works best for you. This may mean that you have to try a few of these to determine what works best for you. Keep in mind that your skills are specific to what feels right for you, so it might be a combination of these and maybe something that is not on the list.

No calls & No texts

I understand that this may be easier said than done and in reality, when you have small children, and elderly parents this may be difficult but not impossible. You should schedule your contact times. Just like when you are out-of-the-office and leave a voicemail, or notification, of who to contact in an emergency. Yes, in these cases you may have to schedule shorter periods but at least you can get a break.

If you need someone to watch an elderly parent, have them contact one of your siblings, a caretaker, or a family friend. If you need someone to watch your child, have them contact your spouse, or child's father, mother, grandparent, etc.

Turn Off Your Computer

Your business will continue to run. Life as you know it will continue. Yes, in some cases work will still pile up but it will be there whether you do it now, or later. I have found that if I wait to respond to some of the emails that I receive -- they will resolve themselves, people will find things that they needed immediately, people will look for themselves, people will ask someone else, and people will take a few minutes to think about what they are asking instead of making YOU their first and only source.

Delegate & Employ Others

- Ask someone else.
- Stay in your area of expertise and giftings.
- Give others a chance to showcase their talents.
- Say No and mean it.
- Don't let others guilt you into doing a task.
- Be careful of the super woman/man cape.

- Watch out for the bait and switch -- taking on a project and you are the only member of the team who consistently shows up.
- Let someone else do it.
- If there is no one else who can do it-then train someone else.
- Crosstrain employees so that you can take a break. This means:
  - Show them how.
  - Teach them how.
  - Do it with them.
  - Observe while they do it.
  - Let them do it.

Yes, discovering emotional wellness and maintaining it is work. But it's so worth it. Most importantly, you are worth it, and once discovered your reality will be transformed!

Reinforcing the Mask: Thoughts and Emotions

Emotional bondage is something that we must set ourselves free from. You may be able to accomplish this on your own, or you may need assistance from professionals in the field of mental health. No matter how you accomplish this, to maintain emotional wellness you will have to manage your thoughts and emotions. In other words, no more masking.

We often struggle because we think we have control over our thoughts and emotions. But our means of control has loopholes that give the enemy access and free reign. When we resist change, we find ourselves in the same place doing the same things day-in and day-out and making no progress and frustrated and discouraged about the lack of progress we are making.

This repetitive circular action is the loop of our existence that is perpetuated by fear and keeps us from moving towards change. The fallacy is the hole that we find ourselves in. The negative emotions that we experience both real and perceived make it difficult to escape this loophole. In biblical terms it is referred to as a trap, snare, or stronghold. Our own thoughts as well as defeating messages that we hear from others keep us bound.

Change is very difficult for many reasons. We talk about thinking positively, read and listen to motivational messages but fail because the most difficult thing to change in life is yourself; you become comfortable operating in dysfunction. Telling yourself "This is the way my life is," "I just have to deal with it," "I am never going to be happy."

There is comfort in knowing the routine, the people, the places; the reality is that staying where you are is easier and more familiar than starting over and facing the unknown. For most of us, negative voices are the loudest and they seem to replay anytime you come face-to-face with the thought of change.

It is difficult to go to a new place in life using an old map (same people telling you what you can't do, what you don't have, what you can't get, who is against you, and constantly reminding you of all your shortcomings). These messages deflate and tear us down, but we have become accustomed to them and made cognitive accommodations to receive them as people looking out for us and out of concern for us.

Removing the mask involves change! After all you have been using the mask to manage your emotions for a while now. A couple of months, years, decades? You have been blinded by the mask for so long that you do not realize that the true happiness that you have been searching for all your life is also being blocked by the mask. If you truly feel defeated but choose to show the world that you are a winner, who are you fooling?

The images you portray to others are just images, not true feelings, because defeat is what's real. Change is not easy. You must ask yourself; what price am I willing to pay for change. Oh, yeah, there's a price. To unmask involves letting go of the unhealthy way of dealing with hurt, pain, grief, despair, guilt, and negative emotions in general. This takes work and commitment.

During the transforming your reality removing the mask workshops, three focus areas are high-lighted because they reinforce and help to maintain emotional wellness. This includes removing the mask, avoiding self-imposed stress, and getting rid of the "noise" *(distractions)* and "clutter" *(things and people that you must let go of)* in our lives so we can fully embrace authenticity.

Emotional Bandwidth: Who's draining my TEE/TEA?

If you're anything like me, you're probably feeling very stressed-out by the state of the world right now. Because of the Internet and 24-hour news channels we are saturated by stories of violence, oppression, political unrest and natural/biological disasters all day and every day.

Watching calamitous events and repeated trauma is exhausting, and it can feel like we're constantly being tormented and feeling overwhelmed. These dangerous images don't dissipate when we turn the television off. No, we internalize them and some impact us more than others. They are housed under the mask and what is under the mask feeds our psyche so that we live in anticipation for the next tragedy.

Emotional bandwidth is a term used to describe the range of emotions that an individual can experience and process effectively. Many of us think that we can handle and cope with different emotional states when in reality, we are just ignoring, hiding, and masking our emotions. When we say, "I'm at my limit!" It's a sign that we've reached the upper end of our emotional bandwidth range. Unfortunately, we do not realize that we have reached this limit until we are there.

When you reach your limits, you can no longer mask. You can't fake happiness anymore, you become irritable, may snap at others, yell, scream and lash out in uncontrollable fits of rage. I have had people in my workshops that say, "I just snapped," "I said things that were out of character for me." In addition, I have had people describe it as an out of body experience. This happens because the mental or emotional state of your current situation has exceeded your ability to mask, handle or process.

When I discuss emotional bandwidth during my speaking engagements, people share that they don't let things bother them and don't understand why they snapped like they did. It is because we are constantly being bombarded by negative stimuli that causes an emotional response. There are situations we experience first-hand, to include traumatic events that impact us directly or indirectly that are stored within your emotional bandwidth. Over time, and depending on the frequency of events, it takes a toll on our mental and emotional health. We can go into overload and start to feel numbed to the pain of others, or on the verge of a nervous breakdown.

Feeling this way should make us stop and slow down, but if we do, we start to feel guilty, or like we are failing or being left behind. What are people going to think if I say "No" if I don't Show, if I do nothing, even worse what will they say? After all, the image others have of you is that you have it all together and your life *(looks)* is perfect. You are that wonderful, loving, caring person, who helps everyone. The fixer, that person that people always want to have in a crisis. Maintaining this image can put you at the top of your emotional bandwidth and lead to a snap!

Maintaining the false images is exhausting work. Riding this rollercoaster will force you to start rationing out your time, energy, and emotions *(TEE)*. Your time will be split and unevenly so in an effort *(energy)* towards maintaining the false images you project to others. This is not a true reflection of how you feel, and more energy is expended to keep true feelings and emotions buried. High-intensity emotions such as anger or anxiety can be tiring and will quickly deplete your energy levels. TEE is used to maintain the image that we want the world to see.

For people you really love *(significant other, lover, children, family etc.)* the acronym is *(TEA)* time, energy, and affection. These acronyms evoke emotions too *(which in a state of depletion, you have a limited supply of)*, and they are guilt and frustration. You feel guilty when you don't have enough TEA for the people in your life who should get more than what you are rationing to others. The problem is that you don't have it to give.

Frustration starts when you know that you are wasting your *(TEE)* on people who will never reciprocate it and will always demand more, which drains and depletes your dwindling supply. It is difficult to get off this rollercoaster because of how we have been educated about emotions and the pressure that comes from society that forces people to establish and maintain an unrealistic state of happiness.

About Emotions

Stop blaming yourself for how you feel or don't feel. If the only emotion that has been reinforced in your life is *Happy*, then that's the emotion you want to show to the world 24/7 and keep everybody *Happy*. My parents were wonderful, and they loved me and my siblings unconditionally, but we rarely discussed emotions except for happy, love, calm-down, fix your face *(mad, upset, unhappy)* and "do you want something to cry for?" *(I know some of you have heard this too!).*

There were people in my life whose faces did not radiate any emotions ever. I always stayed on edge when I was around them because I never knew how they felt about me. Others would make comments like that person didn't let anything bother them, they are tough, they are not afraid of anything, they don't care about anybody, or they're mean as a snake. As I delved into the field of mental health, I learned that what you feel and what you show are two different things so none of those previous statements hold merit.

Then there were those individuals that people warned you about, to stay away from and not to mess with. This would be followed by statements like they haven't been right in the head since the war, or since they lost their child, or some type of tragedy made them "Lose their mind."

It is clear to me now that these individuals suffered from sadness, sorrow, depression, anxiety, or had experienced some break from reality. What I learned and the unspoken message was if you acted this way people will treat you different and call you crazy. In other words, do not let people see this behavior even if you feel this way from time to time. You need to mask these emotions or hide them.

Chapter Takeaways

- We need to teach children about emotions within the family unit, educational system, and it should be a part of a medical wellness check-up from childhood to adulthood.
- It is difficult to be creative or have original thought when your brain is in fight or flight mode 24/7 and your emotions are depleted.
- Connect with people who deposit something positive into your life.
- We live in an age of transactional relationships, so it is important to teach reciprocity.

- Change is not easy, but your emotional free-dom is worth it and most importantly you are worth it.
- Emotional Bandwidth goal... more TEA please!

DO A SELF-CHECK-IN: At various points during the day, ask yourself how you are doing. Are you getting a bit worn out or overwhelmed as the day progresses? Checking in with yourself is a simple strategy to gain perspective on the state of your mental and emotional bandwidth.

Revealing The Authentic You

In this book I have presented various reasons as to why people mask their emotions due to causes such as: cultural influence, no one has modeled behavior that suggest not masking, and no one has discussed or taught how emotions should be handled. But I believe masking, like the layers it creates to reach authenticity, is done for a combination of reasons thereby creating another set of layers that reinforces the mask. Our lack of knowledge and understanding about emotions can lead us to believe that feeling and experiencing certain emotions like depression, sorrow, grief, and others means we have a mental illness, and no one wants to deal with that stigma.

Everyone experiences emotional pain but chooses to mask to keep from further emotional harm, appearing to be weak or vulnerable, or being teased or judged. Gender plays a role in masking. Men may be afraid of compromising their masculinity by showing that they have been hurt in some way, and women don't want to be perceived as being too sensitive and-or not tough enough to survive and-or thrive in a man's world. In general, masking one's feelings is a way to protect yourself from further emotional warfare, and show the world that you are in control of your emotions and-or unphased by a traumatic event. What we are trying to protect by masking our emotions *(ourselves)* harms our emotional well-being and overall mental state.

> It is important that you develop healthy ways of coping with difficult emotions and not be afraid to seek professional support when you need it.

Authenticity

Since unmasking leads to authenticity, it is important that we know who and what we are in search of. According to online sources, authenticity refers to being true to oneself and expressing one's genuine thoughts, feelings, and values. It involves aligning one's actions and behaviors with their inner beliefs and being honest and transparent in interactions with others.

Authenticity is about embracing and accepting one's true self, including both strengths and vulnerabilities, without trying to conform to societal expectations or pretending to be someone else. It involves being genuine, sincere, and consistent in one's words and actions. After hearing this definition, you have to think, who wouldn't want to live this way?

The truth of the matter is that being your authentic self can be challenging for many. People have shared with me that they have a difficult time remembering an authentic version of themselves. I tell them not to feel ashamed. I personally had to go back a couple of decades to find that person and even then, I was trying to live up to someone else's standards. As a part of my workshop, I have attendees define authenticity in their own words and here's some of the feedback I received:

- *Understanding what you value and living by your own set of rules.*
- *Actually being emotionally stable instead of acting like you are.*
- *Freedom to be yourself.*
- *Not being defined by societal roles, expectations, or definitions.*
- *Being genuine.*
- *Understanding my core identity.*

Now that we have a working definition of what lies underneath the mask "authenticity," let's examine reasons for the mask, managing unresolved emotions, the process of unmasking to include pros and cons, a Christian perspective and finally achieving authenticity.

Unresolved Emotions

When we create barriers that prevent us from acknowledging and addressing our true emotions and concerns, several things can happen.

Firstly, these unresolved emotions and concerns don't just go away because we choose to ignore them, they remain right where you buried them. They linger and can manifest as stress, anxiety, or even physical symptoms.

Secondly, by avoiding or suppressing these emotions, we may miss out on other opportunities. We block the full effect of pleasant emotion such as joy, gratitude, serenity, hope, and happiness. We stifle personal growth and self-discovery. More importantly, we don't understand and process our emotions properly, so we don't develop resilience, and our emotional intelligence is lowered.

Lastly, when we are masked, we create a barrier that prohibits the formation of authentic connections with others. When the relationships that you build don't come from an authentic place, then you struggle with issues such as trust, being genuine, and establishing and building meaningful and not superficial relationships. Fostering your true emotions will enhance personal growth, emotional well-being, and healthy relationships.

Process of Unmasking

When you stop masking your emotions and feelings, you can be free to do several things. Firstly, you can be free to express yourself authentically without fear of judgment or rejection. Yes, you will be judged but you will not take it personally. It is impossible to please everybody so stop trying. Focus on you. This will also be difficult at first because other people's happiness has been your priority, but living from an authentic place allows you to fully embrace your true identity and communicate your needs, desires, and boundaries more effectively.

Remember, when you mask, you let others set your boundaries. One of the topics that I discuss as I prepare students to work in the field of human services is burnout. Helping people is a noble profession but the needs can be great, and the numbers of clients served can be many, which can lead to burnout. A major cause of burnout is poor boundaries. Not setting appropriate professional and personal boundaries can lead to exhaustion, depletion, and can impact your emotional bandwidth.

Secondly, you can be free to explore and understand your emotions on a deeper level. No more masking or ignoring them. This self-awareness can lead to personal growth, as you gain insights into your thought patterns, triggers, and areas for improvement.

This third reason is so important: you can be free to make choices and decisions that align with your genuine emotions and values. I can remember struggling to answer questions as simple as *where do you want to eat*? I would take into consideration the group of people I was with, others' food allergies, the distance to a particular restaurant, and a multitude of other factors before I could answer a simple question about where I wanted to eat. By honoring your true feelings, you can pursue paths that fulfill and bring you satisfaction.

Lastly, by not masking your emotions, you can cultivate healthier relationships based on truths, open communications, and emotional intimacy. This can lead to more meaningful connections and a greater sense of belonging. Overall, when you stop masking your emotions and feelings, you can experience a sense of freedom to be your authentic self and live a more fulfilling life.

Several factors can keep someone from being their true authentic self. One common barrier is societal expectations and norms. I shared earlier how society tried to box my son into the image of an athlete based on his height, build, and natural and family history of athleticism. You must understand that society was not your creator and what other people believe is right for you will not always be aligned with the plan God has for your life, Jeremiah 29:11. Yes, it seems easier just to be what society wants you to become because there's acceptance and even reinforcement from family and friends. But this occurs at the expense of your own true happiness and can keep you from your true purpose.

Past experiences and traumas can also play a role in inhibiting authenticity. Negative experiences or conditioning from childhood or previous relationships may lead to a fear of vulnerability or a belief that it is safer to hide one's true self. People have said to me that the thought of having to think about, address, or even discuss certain events from the past was enough by itself to not want to unmask.

In my workshops I have heard people comment, "I never want to go through that on any level again," "let the past stay in the past." Many people stop maturing emotionally when they experience specific traumas in their lives. For example, if something traumatic happened to you at age six, when you are triggered, you will respond emotionally as that traumatized six-year-old instead of the 38-year-old woman that you are.

Emotional age refers to the level of emotional maturity and development that an individual exhibits. It is a concept that suggests that individuals may not always align their emotional responses and behaviors with their chronological age. Emotional age can be influenced by various factors, including life experiences, upbringing, and personal growth.

It is important to note that emotional age is not a fixed or universally defined concept, as emotional development can vary greatly among individuals. Some individuals may exhibit emotional maturity beyond their chronological age, while others may lag behind.

Understanding and assessing emotional age can provide insights into an individual's emotional intelligence, coping mechanisms, and interpersonal skills.

Additionally, personal insecurities and self-doubt make it difficult to trust authenticity. Having low self-esteem or lacking confidence in oneself makes it difficult to embrace or express how you feel, what you think, or even what you really desire. For example, whenever I was with a group of people, I would always wait to hear everyone else's opinion or thoughts before I shared my opinion. When I say, "my opinion," what I would share would be filtered through my mask, carefully shaped, and sometimes contorted to align with the majority with little to no variance.

Low self-esteem refers to a negative perception of oneself and a lack of confidence in one's abilities and worth. I have learned during my many years in mental health that masking creates low self-esteem in people who appear to have the highest levels of confidence.

When someone experiences low self-esteem, they may tend to be hypercritical of themselves, doubt their capabilities and abilities to succeed, and feel unworthy or inadequate. Even if they do not verbalize these insecurities aloud it resonates in their thoughts. This can have various impacts on their life, across social, professional, personal, and work settings. It can even impact overall well-being because low self-esteem can contribute to feelings of anxiety, depression, and social isolation.

When You Take Off the Mask

When you take off the mask self-awareness increases and is no longer inhibited by your negative thoughts or the perceptions of others. By removing the critical spirit that comes with self-doubt you can start to develop self-compassion. I regularly laugh at my mistakes. I know that I am not perfect and ask that people charge the error to my head and not my heart. I remember times when making those same mistakes would have sent me into a spiral of questioning my actions, my abilities, and errors in judgment.

By taking off the mask you will be able to engage in activities that promote self-care, seeking support from trusted individuals, and practicing positive self-talk. It is important to remember that self-esteem can be improved with time and effort, and seeking professional help from therapists or counselors can provide additional guidance and support in this process.

Taking off the mask involves consistently working to overcome any of the previously mentioned obstacles that prevent you from living authentically. What this looks like will differ from person to person but should involve self-reflection *(daily)*, therapy *(personal regiment, breathe-work calming techniques, journaling etc.)*, building a supportive network, and challenging societal expectations.

Embracing authenticity can lead to a greater sense of fulfillment, self-acceptance, and genuine connections with others. In life there are pros and cons. I have found that either side of the continuum involves risks. However, keep in mind that there is a side that involves truth and genuine happiness. No pretending, no masks, emotional wellness and being exactly who God created you to be in this world; but do know, living an authentic life can come with risks and challenges.

When you embrace authenticity, you may experience some of these challenges:

Vulnerability: Being authentic means being open about how we truly feel or think. As a result, people may judge, criticize, or even reject you.

The people who love you for who you are will accept you as you are, including flaws.

Social Disapproval: Living authentically can go
against what society considers to be a norm, or ex-
pectation, creating disapproval from others, po-
tentially impacting our relationships, social standing, or even career opportunities. Remember
much of what is being impacted was built on lies
and false images.

Loss of Relationships: Everybody will not celebrate or appreciate your authenticity. This will be
a time for you to examine your relationships, let
go of people who negatively impact you and gravitate toward those who build, elevate, and positively support you.

Uncertainty and Self-Discovery: There will be
uncertainty especially when what you are seeking
is unknown to you; on the other hand, this can be
very rewarding, learning to accept who you are
and loving who you were created to be.

Christian Perspective

I have held Transforming Your Reality Workshops
at several churches, and I teach at a Christian

university, and put God first and foremost in my life. Throughout this book I have shared that perspective, below is the view my Christian audiences view about masking. It sheds light on why and who is reinforcing the mask as well as what life from a Christian perspective looks like without the mask.

The concept of an "enemy" wanting to keep God's people masked is often discussed in religious or spiritual contexts. It is believed that this "enemy" represents negative or evil forces that aim to hinder spiritual growth and our connection with a higher power. The idea is that by keeping individuals masked or unaware of their true spiritual potential, these forces can prevent them from experiencing the fullness of their faith and the blessings associated with it.

It is important to note that beliefs about the existence and nature of such an enemy vary among different religious and spiritual traditions. Emotions are so important that there are hundreds of verses that address emotions to include specific emotions such as fear, anger, hatred, anxiety, sadness, surprise, joy, hope, and love.

The bible warns us to guard our hearts, mind, and thoughts. We are instructed to renew our minds.

However, as a society we fail to teach, or ensure, that learning about emotions and how to manage them begins early in life. Although there has been some progress, for the most part, mental illness remains a social stigma.

After working with and talking to people who have made the transition and now live from a place of authenticity, they report experiencing the following: *(these experiences can vary from person to person)*

- *Higher self-esteem.*
- *Improved self-confidence.*
- *They enjoy work and experience improved performance.*
- *Great well-being both emotional and physical.*
- *Better relationships.*
- *Experience meaning in life.*
- *Deeper enjoyment and happiness.*
- *Enhanced personal growth.*
- *Better alignment between internal self and outward behavior.*

In conclusion, I want all my readers to experience life to its fullest. I want you each to achieve everything that is bulleted above and more. God created you *to have life, and life more abundantly.* In John

10:10 (NKJV) it reads that in life we all deserve to live what God intended. *The thief does not come except to steal, and to kill, and to destroy. I have come that they may have life, and that they may have it more abundantly.* In the scripture the thief is the "enemy."

About the Author

Transforming Your Reality Removing the Mask is the third book in the training series. Emotional wellness is a concern for everybody; however, Women are the targeted audience because they wear so many different hats! And in reality, layers of Mask. This book will help them break free from the bondage of masking so they can show-up as their authentic self and have the bandwidth to operate at a level of emotional intelligence that allows them to walk in their purpose and be all God created them to be.

The writing style used includes anecdotes and personal stories to help illustrate the phenomenon of masking. The examples provided have been accumulated from educational and work experiences. One of the chapters in the book highlights dichotomous realities, good versus evil; right versus wrong, flesh versus spirit and utilizes the trio of TYRRTM *(transforming your reality removing the mask)* tools to walk readers through the process of experiencing a paradigm shift so they can live in the light of continuous truth and authenticity.

Throughout the book, readers are encouraged to face their own unique reality and elevate to a place in their lives that is uninhibited by any other influence accept their own. Once there, the transition will begin. Each chapter empowers readers to reclaim, remember, and discover their true identity and be at peace with the person within.

More about Dr. Michelle Boone-Thornton

Dr. Michelle Boone-Thornton has worked alongside domestic and international leaders. She is an award-winning international speaker, author, educator, and humanitarian. In 2023, she was appointed World Civility Ambassador by iChange Nations for her global contributions. She is the recipient of the 2022 iChange Nations Astell Collins Generation Leader award and the 2023 Builders Legacy Award. Additionally, in 2023, Dr. Boone-Thornton received the highest honor given by the National Association of Negro Business and Professional Women's Club, the prestigious, Sojourner Truth Award.

Dr. Michelle Boone-Thornton's collegiate education includes a bachelor's degree in social work, a master's degree in Urban Education Guidance and Counseling, and a doctorate in Educational Psychology. She has worked across numerous settings in the field of mental health and held direct services, supervisory, and administrative positions.

Although she worked in residential programs, she thoroughly enjoys community-based settings. She is also a university professor; following in her parents' footsteps, she has championed education from kindergarten through college. Both of her parents were educators. She thoroughly enjoys teaching and is grateful for the opportunity to help students of all ages discover their purpose, uncover gifts and talents, and expand their worldview.

Dr. Boone-Thornton believes that learning is a reciprocal process that creates a natural interactive exchange of ideas, visions, and creativity. It produces a unique opportunity for the teacher and learner to extend personal boundaries, create new constructs, and experience the vulnerability and strength of the human spirit. Dr. Boone-Thornton is a qualified mental health provider in the Commonwealth of Virginia with a specialization in child and adolescent therapies.

She is married to her husband Virgil Thornton Sr., and they have three adult children. They have served as foster parents since 2012, providing both permanent and respite care. Dr. Boone-Thornton wants readers to use The Transforming Your Reality: Removing the Mask workbook, companion journal, and this book to uncover and release emotional turmoil so the light of reality can shine through the cracks of our dismantled mask and allow our true potential to be unleashed.

Appendix *(Mental Health Resources)*

Employee Assistance Program
https://www.indeed.com/career-advice/career-development/employee-assistance-program

Five Stages of Grief
https://www.cnn.com/2021/09/12/health/five-stages-of-grief-kubler-ross-meaning-wellness/index.html

Life Stressor Checklist
https://www.ptsd.va.gov/professional/assessment/documents/LSC-R.pdf

Mental Health First Aid https://www.mentalhealthfirstaid.org/mental-health-resources/

Mental Health. Gov https://www.mentalhealth.gov/

National Alliance on Mental Health
https://www.nami.org/Home

National Institute of Mental Health
https://www.nimh.nih.gov/

National Suicide Prevention Lifeline https://suicidepreventionlifeline.org/ 1-800-273-TALK (8255)

Substance Abuse and Mental Health services Administration
https://www.samhsa.gov/find-help/national-helpline
https://www.samhsa.gov/find-treatment

The Holmes and Rahe Stress Scale: A Self-Assessment to Understand the Impact of Long-Term Stress
https://www.stress.org/holmes-rahe-stress-inventory

Toxic Positivity https://www.medicalnewstoday.com/articles/toxic-positivity

Types of Traumas https://yourexperiencesmatter.com/learning/trauma-stress/types-of-trauma/

Veterans Crisis line https://www.veteranscrisisline.net/

www.ingramcontent.com/pod-product-compliance
Lightning Source LLC
Chambersburg PA
CBHW072203090426
42740CB00012B/2374